W.A.I.T

Women Anticipating an Incredible Turnaround

Dr. Sheila R. Thomas

W.A.I.T

Women Anticipating an Incredible Turnaround

Copyright © 2020 Sheila Thomas

All rights reserved. No part of this book may be reproduced in any form, stored in any retrieval system, or transmitted in any form by any means-electronic, mechanical, photocopy, recording, or otherwise without prior written permission from the publisher.

Published in the United States by Great Day Publishing

WITH GRATITUDE

For my darling Mother, Ethel, who always expected me to succeed, I dedicate this book to you. You are my Shero, a single mother who taught your children to love God and work hard! My Angel, keep watching over me with your loving spirit!

To my foxy grandmother, Daisy, who left a remarkable impression of what wisdom looks like, I thank you. Your love for reading and the ability to recite scriptures with only an 8th-grade education was impressive. I will forever cherish your wisdom.

I could not have done this without the guidance of my editor, Sharai Robin, who pushed me to tell more of the story that she knew I had dwelling inside of me. Thank you for pushing me!

I appreciate my Soror, Erin, for encouraging me and giving constructive criticism that was well needed. You, my dear, are a jewel!

To my dear darling husband, Erick, who pushed me to write this book for over ten years, I thank God for you. Your love and support are what I needed when I wanted to give up. You are my biggest fan!

Finally, with God, all things are possible. Prayer and faith are the tools that enabled me to endure and complete this journey. Lord, I thank you!

TABLE OF CONTENTS

Introduction 1

Chapter One: Waiting for Healing 7

Chapter Two: Waiting for Love and Marriage 27

Chapter Three: Waiting for Success 39

Chapter Four: Waiting for a Financial Breakthrough 51

Final Thoughts 63

W.A.I.T.
Women Anticipating Incredible Turnaround

Introduction

"I Just Want to Be Happy!" I always love listening to this song written by Kirk Franklin. My simple goal in life has always been to be satisfied and contented. Well, I am fabulously 52 and I have finally arrived at my happy place. I no longer struggle with my career. I do not worry about paying the bills. Playing the dating game is over. Depression from physical and emotional pain is in my rearview mirror. I have three handsome sons and a wonderful grandson. My husband is my earthly King, and I know that he treasures me as his Queen. Through God's grace and mercy, we have become as one in every aspect of our lives. We also vow to do whatever is necessary for our spiritual and financial growth. I know that without God, I could do nothing. I put total trust in God and let Him lead and guide my life. I am genuinely happy!

But life has not always been good. Imagine wearing a mask for thirteen years to hide the shame of who you really are. Back in the day, I lived the perfect life for the public. You know the type...., always happy, dressed to the nines, walked like I had it going on and talked as if I was on top of the world. The reality was that my insides were raw and mangled. My heart was aching. It was a bunch of shards and broken pieces. My life felt hopeless and dark.

As the saying goes, *you have not lived unless you have gone through something.* I knew that I was going to have to deal with life issues…but why was it so extreme and painful? My divorce left me bitter and insecure about ever being able to sustain a fruitful relationship. My mom died when I was twenty-seven years old, and I carried that void in my heart. I even questioned my intelligence because I rarely got any of the jobs I desired. Then, there was the stress of living from paycheck to paycheck. I thought that I was being the perfect bag lady, carrying all my baggage well. Only until it kept piling on my shoulders, and I began to crumble. Stress can be a primary source of sickness. Being so emotionally drained led to physical stress within my body. Sickness began to invade in the form of recurring sinus infections and severe joint pains. I thought all was left to do was to quit working and sit at home. This smart, educated woman to the outside was actually a *pretty mess*!

My husband tried to help pull me through with consolation and prayer. That just was not enough. I had hidden and masked so much until what he gave only scratched the surface of what I needed to bring me back into balance and out of the darkness.

I played the flute in grade school and have always loved music. Music seems to take my mind off the troubles of the world. The melodies and words of songs provide comfort. While in my low state, I started paying closer attention to the lyrics in worship music. Most of these songs contained scriptures and affirmations that pierced my heart and soul. Music became my solace. I found comfort by listening to the words in songs such as Yolanda Adams', "This Battle is not Yours" and Marvin Sapp's "Never Would Have Made It." This all led to me increasing my belief that God can make my life better. I have always prayed; however, believe me when I say that my prayer life grew to another level. I started talking to God more than just during my morning meditation. We started having conversations throughout the day and night. My connection to God through music and prayer brought me out of my dark place and into the waiting room for my turnaround.

Fast forward to today: Now, my sad days have turned around to days of peace, joy and contentment. I no longer allow situations in life to cause me to spiral into a state of despair. I am content like Paul in Philippians 4:11 (K.J.V.) where he stated "Not that I speak in respect of want; for I have learned, in whatsoever state I am, therewith to be content." My contentment does not mean that I am not still striving for success or setting goals. It means that I now have a sense of peace in my soul and heart that comes from knowing who God is and that He is in control of my life. My faith has gotten stronger, and I have learned to pray and not worry.

I desire for everyone who reads this book to enter a place of peace and contentment.

Women Anticipating Incredible Turnaround (W.A.I.T.) are stories about areas in life that women may struggle to move forward or do not believe they can conquer obstacles. This is written as a testament to painful situations that have occurred in my life or the life of friends and family. It tells of how we have experienced a significant turnaround. This is what waiting looks like. Patience and prayer are the keys that I needed to move through hardships and pains and exit the waiting room. Hopefully, after reading this, you can see what waiting looks like. I pray that these experiences will help you to learn to give your burdens to God and stop worrying. I hope that after reading these stories, they will point you in the direction to let God take control of every situation in your life.

God declares that our latter will be greater and that He will grant us peace if we wait in anticipation for an incredible turnaround. It is written in Job 8:7, "Though thy beginning was small, yet thy latter end should significantly increase." This means that as you wait, realize that God has something in store for you that is so big, it will blow your mind!

The waiting room in life can be a place of struggle, strife, insecurity and uncertainty. There will come a time in life when all things seem to be falling apart, and God seems to be nowhere in sight. Trust me; everyone will enter the waiting room at some point in life. However, breaking out of this room and entering the oasis of contentment and peace starts with changing your mindset and trusting the process. You have got to believe that God has a perfect plan in store. Waiting can take months or years. However, you must believe in your heart that God is working things out for you. Remember that in Jeremiah 29:11 the scripture states, "He has made a promise to prosper us and not harm as well as to give us hope and a future."

While you are waiting, know that delay does not always mean denied. Rebuke the distractions of being anxious, feeling frustrated or doubting that the "it" will never happen. In Philippians 4:6-7, God tells us not to be anxious for anything because if we present our requests to Him, He will supply all our needs according to His riches in glory.

Do not let that heavy baggage of physical and emotional pain weigh you down. Wait and Anticipate your Incredible Turnaround!

Do not let previous "No's" stop you from applying for a new job. Keep applying and interviewing as you Wait and Anticipate your Incredible Turnaround!

Do not give up on love and marriage. Prepare your mind, body and soul before you meet that special person. Wait and Anticipate your Incredible Turnaround!

Do not get discouraged about your finances. Keep looking for a financial breakthrough by decreeing and declaring increase, wealth and prosperity every day as you Wait and Anticipate your Incredible Turnaround.

We never know how our story will end or how God will fulfill His promises, but in Proverbs 3:5-6 (K.J.V.), we are told to, "Trust in the Lord with all thine heart; and lean not unto thy own understanding. In all thy ways acknowledge Him, and He shall direct thy paths." **W**omen must trust the process and **A**nticipate an **I**ncredible **T**urnaround!

Chapter 1: Waiting for Healing

Scars are the indelible imprints on the body or hidden memories caused by a type of physical or emotional pain or trauma. It is natural to wonder how long it will take for scars to heal, and when will they ever fade away. How do you treat your scars? Do you tend to them with care to aid the healing, or do you allow the scars to fester by not providing the care needed to heal? You have a choice. You can either embrace them as marks of beauty and triumph or agonize over them as disfigurements to your body and soul. Regardless of what kind of scar, it can be thought of as a sore, and we know that all wounds go through a process of healing.

The healing process makes the body or mind healthy again. God will sometimes place us in a waiting room for healing. This waiting room is a time in life when all things seem to be falling apart, and God seems to be nowhere in sight. God works to heal us while we are in the waiting room. Trust me, do not be surprised if it happens differently than you expected. The stories in this chapter attest to how God demonstrates for us His love, power and protection while in the waiting room. One story tells how my niece battled cancer and now has become a voice of care and understanding for women her age who are struggling. My story is one that reveals how God healed my hurt in an unexpected way.

The Physical Healing Waiting Room

Repairing a damaged body to its normal function is physical healing. A person's body may need to heal from bumps, scrapes, and bruises, or internal damage such as arthritis, stroke or cancer. Physical damage may leave visible scars such as blemishes or spots on the outside of the body as well or disfigurements and scars inside the body. It doesn't matter if the scars from physical damage can be seen or not; once an injury occurs, a healing process must take place. The process of healing inside or outside may be short or extensive, but a person must be patient for the body to heal.

I witnessed the process of physical and emotional healing with my niece and her fight with cancer. I would have never thought my niece, Tifanie, would be diagnosed with cancer at such a young age. She was in the prime of her life and living life to the fullest. She had recently bought a house, was setting goals to become a real estate agent, travel more and do everything possible so that she and her daughter could have a good life. She was getting things done and checking them off her list. Life was going fine, but her plans took an abrupt halt! During a time when she enjoyed celebrating life most, which was her birthday month, she received the devastating diagnosis.

One cold day in December, she felt a mass in her breast. She went to the doctor to have it examined. Stage I breast cancer was the report that she later received...*Devastation, Anger...Could this really be happening?* She felt as if her life was being ripped apart.

These were her thoughts written in her journal:

"You have breast cancer. The four dreadful words any woman fears hearing. I was devastated. I was torn. I was broken! How did this happen? Am I going to die? Who's going to raise my daughter? A million questions were racing through my mind while trying to keep my composure, and most importantly, being strong for my mom so that she wouldn't lose it. January 8, 2019, would be the turning point that dictated the rest of my life! The fear of the unknown, the aches and pain, the treatment stripping me down to my barest form. I was broken! I was hurt!"

This beast, *Cancer*, was not part of her life plan. No way. She was too young, the mother of a preteen daughter, a future real estate agent and, most importantly, a Christian woman. She had recently committed her life to trust God more and do what was in His will and His way! She had asked God to reveal Himself in a powerful way as a testament to her faith and ability to trust in Him. She never expected Him to fulfill her request for a testament to manifest this way!

Cancer came like a thief, attacking her body, mind and spirit. Cancer transformed my niece from an independent woman who was head of her household, to one who had to depend on others just to make it through the day. Think about it. She was used to paying her bills, raising her daughter and grinding from 8 to 5 daily. The agony during this tedious journey also had its share of aches and pains including bruises from needles, surgical cuts and chemotherapy. The physical pain and the mental drain were sometimes too much to bear and led to occasional anger and bitterness. There were times when managing life tasks such as driving to appointments, taking care of her daughter, draining her wounds, preparing or running out to get meals were just too much. She felt like she was fighting alone. Often, she prayed, cried, screamed and hollered, seeking relief from this burden she was carrying. Many times, she asked, "Why me, Lord?" Sometimes, He answered her. However, there were also times when she felt as if He wasn't listening. Her hopelessness and feelings of despair were often overwhelming.

I gained a different perspective on the waiting process of physical healing from seeing my niece in such misery. I took an active role in her journey of healing as a caretaker, confidant, shoulder to cry on, and nurturer through phone calls and FaceTime. During the process of healing, my niece looked for support from friends and family. At first, their support poured in heavily. After a few months, the phone calls and visits became little to none. Much of the disconnection was due to family and friends having never gone through cancer or a life-threatening disease, and not being able to comprehend the intensity of it all entirely.

We did not understand why she was happy some days and why on other days, she refused to talk.

I was not used to how my niece was behaving. She called me often to talk or vent. She wanted me just to listen and not give advice. Listening was easy, but not being able to give my two cents was hard. My advice included things I thought she should do for her health and well-being, and also on issues such as parenting and her relationship with others. She did not want to hear my unsolicited advice which eventually created a wedge in our close relationship. Our phone conversations eventually became daily disagreements full of short and snappy words.

We were colliding so much. My advice to her was to pray more and continue to find strength in God and His word. I also suggested that she find someone who would better understand what she was going through. I felt that she could relate better to other breast cancer survivors. I am so thankful that she took my advice and reached out to other women who had breast cancer. She formed bonds that led to some fantastic friendships with her "breasties." They talked almost every day. Now, they are her prayer partners, travel buddies and spirit lifters! The joy that my niece had when she spoke of her breasties, brought me a sense of peace because I knew that she had people close to her who understood what she was going through. Her relationship with her breasties reminds me of Ecclesiastes 4:9-10: "Two are better than one because they have a good return for their labor: If either of them falls down, one can help the other up. But pity anyone who falls and has no one to help them up." My niece realized that these ladies were a Godsend because her breasties understood her fears and tears.

Today, my niece is a prayer warrior, leaning, and depending on God for total restoration of her mind, body and soul after her bout with cancer. She spends her time waiting for healing in prayer, volunteering, and doing something she loves, which is traveling. She has taken a trip to Jamaica and Las Vegas to immerse herself in new scenery with company that gives her peace, strength and solace. She keeps a journal of her battle and is working on a Vlog to share her story with others. Her hope is that she can help others through the ordeal with information she couldn't find for herself but learned along the way. The journey of my niece's healing is often full of pain, tears and laughter. One of her quotes that keep her inspired is, "You are *Braver* than you believe, *Stronger* than you seem, and *Smarter* than you think."

My niece and I have a beautiful relationship again. I am patient, more compassionate and considerate of what she has been through. In turn, she also takes time to explain how she is feeling so I can gain a better understanding of her journey. I wrote the following poem which is my perspective of the things my niece was going through:

Tifanie's Journey

The journey has been rough with my tits
Some days it drives me out of my wits
But I am not going to let cancer win I
will be a champion to the end.

Some days I feel like giving up
I say Lord take away this cup I
have so much more to do Lord,
I will continue to trust you.

People call and don't know what to say
I wish they would leave me alone and pray
I am not mean; it's just how I feel Some
days I just have to keep it real.

Not saying that I am always right
But this journey has been a fight
Dealing with pain hour after hour Can
make my attitude a little sour.

Some days I would love to go on an outing
To release my spirit of fret and doubting
I love my life and know I'll be okay
Thank you for helping me make it day after day!

Tifanie has proven to be a woman of strength. A year and a half later, she now shares this beautiful testimony from her journey:

"Fast forward to June 25, 2020, in the middle of a damn pandemic and a war on humanity, and I'm thriving through all of the bullshit! Who knew I have been reconstructed and beautifully put back together, stronger than ever? I never had a self-esteem issue with my appearance and complexion, but damn, I never knew I could love myself 10x more after breast cancer. Embracing the scars and all. My body is a work of art, a beautiful showcase that tells my story and how God can take nothing and mold it into something. 'And we know that in all things God works for the good of those who love him, who have been called according to His purpose' (Romans 8:28). His good, His glory! Breast cancer just may have been my biggest blessing yet!"

Waiting on God for physical healing was a time of discovery for my niece. She spent many days alone, and in this quiet space, she was able to hear from God on matters such as her health, career, relationships and parenting. She has discovered that life is worth living, and she is taking advantage of it every day. Although she has reached some normalcy in her life, the days when her life seems frazzled from physical pain and overwhelming emotions, she remembers that God is always there to carry her burdens. The Bible tells us in 1 Peter 5:6-7(K.J.V.) to be humble under His mighty hand and to cast our cares on Him because He will exalt us. God continues to give her peace through prayer, journaling and reading scriptures.

Losing faith when pain is racking your body can happen, but God gives us great assurance that we can depend on Him. There are several stories in the Bible, where He provided a healing touch to His people. For example, Mark 6:56 (N.I.V.) states, "And wherever he went—into villages, towns or countryside—they placed the sick in the marketplaces. They begged him to let them touch even the edge of his cloak, and all who touched it were healed."

God offers grace and mercy to everyone. God does not expect us to be happy about the situation that changed us physically, but He does expect us to trust Him to be a comforter and healer.

Pray these prayers of faith while you are in the physical waiting room:

Have mercy upon me, O Lord; for I am weak: O Lord, heal me; for my bones are vexed. Psalms 6:2 (K.J.V.)

But he was wounded for our transgressions, he was bruised for our iniquities: the chastisement of our peace was upon him, and with his stripes, we are healed. Isaiah 53:4-6 (K.J.V.)

Heal me, O LORD, and I shall be healed; save me, and I shall be saved: for thou art my praise. Jeremiah 17:14 (K.J.V.)

The Waiting Room of Emotional Healing

I entered the emotional healing waiting room with the loss from my mom when I was twenty-seven years young. My mother was my Shero. She was a Christian woman full of grace, beauty, charm and intellect. For over thirty years, she worked as a nurse on the night shift. Nurturing others back to good health was her passion. I looked forward to her morning phone calls checking on my son and me before we went to school and work.

One beautiful bright morning in May, my mom and I had our usual early morning phone conversation. She would call each morning around 7:00 a.m. before she left the night shift at the hospital to make sure my son and I were up and ready for school. I always looked forward to these conversations. In turn, I would call her daily at 4:00 p.m. before leaving work to see if she needed anything from the store before I arrived to pick up my son from her home. I would have never thought that this would be the last conversation we would ever have.

Thirty minutes later, as I arrived at my job, I received a call that my mom had been in an accident. That phone call was devastating. My sister-in-law was the one who called since she was a police dispatcher and had received the

information firsthand. Although she was telling me to listen and remain calm, I could hear the anxiety in her voice. I knew right then and there that this was serious.
My thoughts were everywhere…My mom had just left work, and I had just spoken with her. How could this have happened? I was agitated, perplexed and totally confused while standing there listening to my sister-in-law. I now recall just holding the phone and saying repeatedly, "NO, NO, NO!"

My principal had to drive me to the hospital. When I arrived, I could feel the sting in the air that all was not well. As I walked into the waiting area where my sister and grandmother were, their faces expressed a sense of worry. They were upset and crying. My grandmother was distraught. She had just lost her sister only five days ago, and now her only child was in a state of unconsciousness. We all were in a state of disbelief. My mom had suffered a cerebral hemorrhage while driving and ran into a tree. This accident happened not even a mile from her house.

Mom remained in a coma for what seemed like an eternity. It was only for three days. On that third day, God sent a sign to let me know that my mom was about to leave us. Her favorite color was blue, and a bluebird was outside my window that beautiful Friday morning, and as I watched it, it looked at me and flew away. I understood the sign that God had given me at that moment and asked Him to give me strength. Later that evening, my mom took her last breath.

Losing my mom at an early age left a scar on my heart that I thought would never heal. She and I had formed a loving relationship. Although I did not often cook, when I did, I could always call her for tips and ideas. She provided sound advice on parenting. She was there to comfort me and give me guidance during my divorce. She believed in education and was overjoyed when I completed my master's degree. Although she wasn't alive when I finished my Specialist and Doctorate degrees, I could feel her presence and visualize her warm smile as I marched across the stage. Her sudden death left me numb for many years, whereas I found it hard to attend funerals or visit loved ones in the hospital. I was in a place as described in the book of Psalms 119:28 (N.I.V.), "My soul is weary with sorrow; strengthen me according to your word."

It took years to shake off the feeling of emptiness. I did not talk about my feelings of sadness, mainly because I wanted to be strong for my son. But every song I heard that reminded me of her caused me to break down and cry. I refused to attend church on Mother's Day for years because of the sadness it would bring to see others there with their moms. However, my restoration started when I had to fill in the gap when of my best friend's mom was ill. She and I have been friends for over thirty years. Throughout the years, we were each other's support. Although we leaned on each other in times of need, I never expected to be placed in the position to tend to her mom on her sickbed.

Like my mom, Mrs. Davis's illness and death were sudden. She was also a vibrant Christian woman like my mom, retired and living life to the fullest. I can vividly remember the day my friend Ericka called. She was worried and asked me to go to the hospital to check on her mom. Ericka lived almost three hours away. As an only child, she did not have anyone else to check on her mom, and as her best friend, she knew I would stand in the gap for her.

When she asked me to go to the hospital, I hesitated a little. I am sure she did not notice. How could I go to THAT hospital that did not save my mother? I made a vow that the only way that I would go back to THAT hospital would be an emergency with my husband, children or an immediate family member! A hospital was a place of doom and gloom. It was the last place that I had seen the person who had taken care of me for twenty-seven years. I was mad at everyone at THAT hospital.

I shared the news with my husband. He knew how hard this task would be for me. He even said, "I know it's hard, but baby, you've got to go for your friend." I did not want to hear that. Why didn't he say that he would see if he could find someone else to go for me or something along those lines? Perhaps even, "Sweetie, what are you feeling?" His words upset me even more. Not only did he tell me I had to go, but he also stated that I had to go alone. He was not going with me because we could not take our young son. *What? Are you kidding me?* He did offer to pray for Mrs. Davis and me before I left. Although it was still not what I wanted, my husband's prayer provided some comfort.

Really God? You put me in a position to think about someone else's needs? I had to quickly realize that it was not about me and my feelings. Ericka was in need, and I had to be there for her. Although I was in the emotional healing waiting room, I had to get over myself and help someone else.

As I drove to the hospital, I was overflowing with anxiety. What was her mom's state? Could I stay strong enough even to fill in the gap? Could I relay any vital medical information to Ericka? As I dragged my body inside the hospital and to Mrs. Davis's room, I kept praying for the Lord to give me strength. My plea was these simple words, "Help me, Lord." Once I entered the hospital room, I felt a strange surge of energy. It was like a new awakening. I had the confidence to complete this task. I knew that the Lord had given me this newfound strength. Immediately, I felt like I was starting the journey to heal my emotional pain! My wait for emotional healing was almost over. I was standing in the gap for someone else. I was so thankful that God had given me the courage and strength to fill this gap. Now, it was time for the next test.

The scene was the same as when my mom was in the hospital. The reeking smell of blood, the beep of the monitors, as well as the sight of her lying in that hospital bed brought back horrible memories. Mrs. Davis was even lying in the same position as my mom. The only difference was that her mom was conscious. I kept saying in my mind, "Okay, God. Help me through this." Ericka needs me, and I have got to do this. At that point, I decided not to let my emotions overcome the situation. Instead, I leaned over to kiss and hug Mrs. Davis. I told her that I would be there until Ericka could make it. The few hours that I was there felt like an eternity. I prayed the same plea repeatedly, "Help me, Lord," and He answered my prayers. I was able to provide comfort to Mrs. Davis and communicate the medical information to Ericka.

Like I said earlier, the emotional healing journey had just begun. I thought that I had this beat. Unbeknownst to me, my work wasn't quite finished. You see, not soon after this ordeal, Mrs. Davis passed away. I had to face more grief. Ericka asked me to help plan and execute some of the arrangements for the homegoing service. *Really?* I mean, this is supposed to be a journey of healing. This is not supposed to be an emotional roller-coaster. *Did Ericka really expect me to go through this again? How in the world was I supposed to help her when I had just buried my mom not long ago?* Still, I had to dust myself off, move out of the way and plead once again to the Lord to give me strength. "Lord, have mercy on me!"

God gave me the strength to be a comfort and show care and love to my friend during her time of loss. While in the waiting room for my healing, I found myself unselfishly serving another. Standing in the gap for my friend brought closure for me from my mother's death and the healing I needed to return to a state of joy and peace in my life. Being there for my friend helped me to realize that I am stronger than I thought. It was a hefty challenge to tend to her mom during her sickness and also to help prepare for her funeral, but I was able to complete the challenge. It was tough, but by crying out for help to God, I was able to withstand. God heard my cries for help during both situations with my friend's mom. By spending my time caring for and serving others, God healed me from the pain of losing my mom. I am now able to talk about my mom's death more without getting sad. Mother's Day is still lonely without her, but I can now attend church and not be saddened when others are there with their moms.

While you are waiting on your physical or emotional healing, do not be discouraged. Just know that God provides healing from the physical scars that wreak havoc on the body and the emotional scars that tear our heart and soul to pieces. For healing to happen, there may be a need to find solace in someone who better understands what you need. You may also find healing by serving others. While you wait, there may be someone who needs your help, which is one of God's ways of giving you a renewed mind and spirit.

The waiting room to heal may be a dreary, painful place, but if we put our trust in the Lord while there and remember that He has left us a Comforter of peace, it will make the waiting more comfortable to endure. This waiting process needs to take place in order to grow and learn and receive the blessings God has in store for us. Engaging in daily prayer and studying God's word increases our endurance and strengthens us. Do not waste time while in the waiting room; instead, use this time to draw closer to God. God's delay does not mean denial for His blessings are on the way.

As you linger in the waiting room for healing, read and meditate on the following scriptures:

Heal me, O Lord, and I will be healed; save me, and I will be saved, for you are the one I praise. Jeremiah 17:14 (N.I.V.)

Dear friend, I pray that you may enjoy good health and that all may go well with you, even as your soul is getting along well. 3 John 1:2 (N.I.V.)

But I will restore you to health and heal your wounds, declares the LORD. Jeremiah 30:17 (N.I.V.)

Have mercy on me, LORD, for I am faint; heal me, LORD, for my bones are in agony. Psalms 6:2 (N.I.V.)

LORD my God, I called to you for help, and you healed me. Psalms 30:2

I have seen their ways, but I will heal them; I will guide them and restore comfort to Israel's mourners, creating praise on their lips. Peace, peace, to those far and near, says the LORD. And I will heal them. Isaiah 57:18-19 (N.I.V.)

He gives strength to the weary and increases the power of the weak. Isaiah 40:29 (N.I.V.)

He heals the brokenhearted and binds up their wounds. Psalms 147:3 (N.I.V.)

Casting all your care upon him; for he careth for you. 1 Peter 5:7

Prayer for Healing

Heavenly Father, I come humbly before You, asking You to heal me in every area of my life. I need healing for emotional hurts and physical pains that hinder my wellbeing. I kneel before You, knowing that You have the power and might to make all things well again. I ask that you make my heart whole again from the pains of losing a loved one or from rejections of others. You have all the power to heal the aches and pains that flow through my body. There are things I do not understand, but I have faith and believe that You can and will heal me. I trust in You for healing and will give you all the praise and glory for your marvelous works. Help me, Lord! In the Mighty name of Jesus, I pray. Amen.

Jot down why you are in the waiting room for healing? Which Bible verse do you find most comforting above for your healing, and why?

_____

_____

_____

_____

_____

_____

_____

_____

_____

_____

_____

_____

_____

_____

Chapter 2: Waiting for Love and Marriage

Most women have a longing or desire to be loved and wanted by that special someone. We were all little girls, imagining that our prince would come to sweep us off our feet. I spent my teenage years imagining my life as a wife and mother. I even planned out all the specifics of my dream wedding, including, when I would get married, the color and types of flowers, who my bridesmaids would be, the venue for the reception and the honeymoon destination. In my mind, it was a beautiful plan, but things didn't quite go as I had envisioned. You see, I thought my prince was my high school sweetheart, a person I had been in love with for many years. I thought I was his pretty princess and that he would fulfill my dreams for a beautiful wedding, healthy marriage and becoming a mother. But it all did not quite happen that way. Here is my story.

As I was completing my final classes to become a teacher, my high school sweetheart and I found out that we were having a baby. I was excited but scared. I was not sure if I would be able to find a teaching position since I was pregnant. However, I was still excited because my plan was still moving forward; I was marrying my prince. Yes, there was a wedding, and my colors and flowers were included BUT, there was no honeymoon, and the timing was off. I will talk more about the timing later. Eventually,

I was offered a teaching position. Life was good! The guy that I had literally fought for in high school had now become my husband. I thought that I had finally finished the battle for love and would enjoy this new phase of my life.

Well, my dream for a happy home was quickly diminished when my husband was called to serve in Desert Storm. We had only been married for five months, and the baby was due in a few weeks. He ended up leaving for war training during the last few weeks of my pregnancy. I was crushed. Here I was a newlywed, a brand-new teacher and living alone for the first time in my life. This was not what I had envisioned. Instead of being joyful about it all, I was now sad and sometimes angry. This is not what I had prayed for. During the call to war, a soldier was not able to call home often, and whenever my husband did call, it was a brief conversation. It was a rough time for me. He was not sure if he would even be able to come home for our son's birth. My dream of the happy couple at the hospital awaiting the arrival of the baby was shattered!

Our son was three months old before my husband returned home. I was delighted for his return, but the time apart seemed to cause a wedge in the relationship. It seemed as if he had lost interest in me. Our sex life was almost nonexistent. He did not spend much time at home when he wasn't working. Of course, this had me wondering if it was me or did something happen while he was gone that turned his love and attention away from me.

In my opinion, our marriage seemed odd. There was no romance or date nights. We were living in the household as roommates instead of husband and wife. Like roommates, we split all the bills. I attended church alone while he partied most nights when he was not at work. Our son would often ask where his dad was, and I would answer with a response that he was at work or just busy. Our parenting skills were also different. He was extremely strict and I was a nurturer. We were not a perfect fit according to the scripture found in 2 Corinthians 6:14, which reads, "Do not be unequally yoked together with unbelievers. For what fellowship has righteousness with lawlessness." Instead of working together, we were at odds with one another. Our belief systems were not the same, and it did not seem that our lives were heading in the same direction. I did not feel any type of love from him, and my love for him was slowly fading away. I stayed in the marriage for five long years, many of which I felt all alone and broken. The only joy in my home was my son. This marriage lasted five years and left me heartbroken and bitter.

After the marriage ended, I found myself in the waiting room for love. I had a strong desire for someone to fill the void of loneliness. I read self-help books to learn what to do while waiting for love. Praying and begging God to send someone was a daily ritual. I sought the advice of friends and family on how to find a mate, and what they thought went wrong with the marriage. It seemed as if no one or nothing could help fill the void in my heart. Soon, I began to lose heart, and my faith began to waver. I felt like giving up on ever finding love again.

I eventually decided to apply Psalm 27:14 (K.J.V.) to my situation, "Wait on the Lord, be of good courage, and He shall strengthen your heart; Wait, I say on the Lord." I would have never thought that my time of waiting would become a nine-year journey. The struggle was real. I was not able to make a connection with most guys because of the bitterness I harbored from my first marriage. I felt that all men would break my heart; therefore, I became mean and heartless. I dated but chose not to get emotionally tied down.

Eventually, I realized that my attitude towards dating and men was not Godly. I knew that for God to send love my way, I had to change my mindset and patiently wait for Him to send me my soulmate. I knew my worth and value and decided to be patient until the right person came along who would value me as much as God did. I was a lady who was waiting for love, waiting for God to send the man he had chosen for me.

While waiting, I decided to focus on myself. My heart yearned for someone special to spend my time with, but instead of dwelling on what I didn't have, I chose to trust and wait on God for my mate and be grateful for the people and things in my life at that moment. Yes, I wanted a mate, and some days were cold and lonely, but I learned to fix my mind on other things. Raising my son and assuring that his future was bright became my priority. I did things to increase my character, capacity, capability and abilities. God is the best Human Resources Manager, giving the best jobs for each person. My roles included parenting my young son, using my gifts at church with youth ministry and the choir and increasing my knowledge by obtaining another degree. Love and marriage were no longer at the forefront of my thinking. I decided to mount up on God's word daily, immersing myself with positive scriptures and songs of aspiration for my soul. I often prayed for love to happen while focusing on my personal growth and my son. During this time of self-fulfillment and reflection, God gave me a new vision and hope for my future.

At the age of 30, I had a vision and purpose set for my life. I had given myself a deadline of 35 to find love again, get married, have another child and buy a house. I desired someone to love me, treat my son as his own and take out the trash. I was a focused and goal-oriented educator, planning my next steps, which were to obtain a doctoral degree in educational leadership and another master's degree in school counseling. I desired a husband but was enjoying the single life as well. It was just my son and me against the world, and no one or nothing could stop us. I knew my worth and value and chose to be patient until the right person came along who would value me as much as my God. After three years of waiting and soul searching, it occurred to me that God needed to repair my broken heart and deflated spirit while he was getting my soulmate ready for me.

While waiting, I discovered that I needed an attitude adjustment to make space for my soulmate. I had become the woman who thought she did not need a man to complete her. I was doing well financially and did not have the patience or time to deal with a man who wanted to play games. I had concluded that my soulmate was far away and that we would never connect. But a part of me still trusted in the words that God has declared in Genesis 2:18 (N.I.V.), that it is not good for man to be alone. I kept a little faith and believed His words that there had to be someone out there in this world that He created just for me.

Oddly enough, my soulmate was right in the same city and had mutual friends and associates, but our paths never crossed. By the age of 34, I had just about given up on marriage. Then, a close friend decided she wanted to play a love connection by introducing me to her and her husband's friend.

The story of our connection is a sweet one. As she described him to me, he sounded a little interesting. She said he was a hard worker, a few years older than me, handsome and a Christian. He met my mental checklist for the characteristics of a "good man." When she stated that he was a preacher, I was a little taken aback. I mean, the thoughts of dating a minister weren't because I didn't believe in God; I just wondered if he would understand that although I love Jesus, I also had a passion for music, wine and dancing.

For two weeks, my friend labored in prayer until she heard from God that the timing was right to make the connection. We were finally "hooked up" and had our first phone conversation. This phone call was the beginning of a 6-month whirlwind romance. I entered this relationship with a guarded heart. I made a vow not to fall too deep and end up getting hurt. Wait a minute! There was something different about this guy. He knew when to call, what to say and how to say it. He respected my time with my son, and when I needed rest. Have you ever thought of someone being too perfect? Well, he was almost too perfect for me. I was so scared. I found myself falling in love within two weeks. Not me, "Ms. Hardcore!"

I now realize that God's divine intervention is what brought us together after we both adjusted our attitudes and thoughts. I was a cold-hearted woman, guarding and protecting my heart. He was a man who had also been hurt and had dealt with other pains in life; therefore, he moved cautiously before entering a new relationship. Once God fixed our hearts and minds, we were ready for love. It is then that He decided to bring forth a union that has withstood many tests and trials.

I am no longer a Woman in Waiting! I derived from my husband's rib and am now his helpmate, standing behind him to hold him up when he falls. My husband follows the scripture in Ephesians 5:32, "Husbands, love your wives, even as Christ also loved the church, and gave himself for it." He is attentive, nurturing, caring and understanding. God has given me the desires of my heart after a long period of waiting. His timing was not mine because I did not know the plans He had for me concerning my mate. I know He has given me a good and perfect gift with my husband because he treats me in a loving way.

You are a beautiful treasure and must be viewed and pursued as such. Wait for God to place the right person in your life who will value you just as He does. You are worthy! Waiting is hard, but don't think of it as a time of loneliness. Spend this time getting to know Jesus and more about yourself. God will hide and protect you from those who seek to harm you. The waiting room for marriage can be a cold and lonely place, but once the door opens, and God allows the right person into your life, your heart and soul will rejoice with gladness. Always remember that you are worth the wait. You are the apple of God's eye, and He only wants what is best for you. He will make all things great and marvelous for you if you patiently wait and trust the process.

Love and marriage are areas where most women seem to linger in the waiting room for an extended time. Marriage for some women makes them feel whole and complete. It fills a void and fulfills the desires of the heart for happiness. Love and marriage can be such a beautiful thing once you connect with the one God has planned for you. Until this connection happens, it is a game of trial and error, a cycle of good and bad dates and relationships. Wait for an Incredible Turnaround regarding marriage and let God's will and God's way take hold. During the time of waiting, you must be very patient and find your purpose. The waiting period is a time for maturity where you should use this time to discover who you are, work toward and achieve your goals and plan for your future. While waiting in full expectation for what God will do, you must fully surrender your heart to God and allow His will to be done. This surrender is a willingness to allow God to strengthen your character, talents, skills and abilities. Choose to trust God for what He has in store for you. He is preparing His promise for you for a mate, but do not rush Him. In your rush, you may not receive the right package that He has for you. Be patient and trust the process. I can attest that once I fully relied and waited on God, He connected me to my soulmate, and this union has been happy ever after.

If you are longing for love or a husband and tired of waiting, I hope these verses and prayer encourage your soul and comfort for your needs in your waiting room.

An unmarried woman or virgin is concerned about the Lord's affairs: Her aim is to be devoted to the Lord in both body and spirit. But a married woman is concerned about the affairs of this world--how she can please her husband.
1 Corinthians 7:34 (N.I.V.)

Delight thyself also in the LORD, and he shall give thee the desires of thine heart. Psalms 37:4 (K.J.V.)

Be ye not unequally yoked together with unbelievers: for what fellowship hath righteousness with unrighteousness? and what communion hath light with darkness? 2 Corinthians 6:14 (K.J.V.)

Whoso findeth a wife findeth a good thing and obtaineth favour of the LORD. Proverbs 18:2 (K.J.V.)

I charge you, O daughters of Jerusalem, that ye stir not up, nor awake my love, until he please. Song of Solomon 8:4 (K.J.V.)

Two are better than one; because they have a good reward for their labour. For if they fall, the one will lift up his fellow: but woe to him that is alone when he falleth; for he hath not another to help him up. Again, if two lie together, then they have heat: but how can one be warm alone? And if one prevails against him, two shall withstand him; and a threefold cord is not quickly broken. Ecclesiastes 4:9-12 (K.J.V.)

Who can find a virtuous woman? for her price is far above rubies. Proverbs 31:10 (K.J.V.)

And the LORD God said, It is not good that the man should be alone; I will make him an help meet for him. Genesis 2:18 (K.J.V.)

Ask and it will be given to you; seek and you will find; knock and the door will be opened to you. Matthew 7:7 (N.I.V.)

Prayer for Love and Marriage

Lord, I trust and believe that in your perfect timing, you will bless me with my soulmate. I ask that you strengthen my faith and patience during this time of waiting. I will wait joyfully on the excellent plan you have for my life. I pray for peace in my heart to ease this weight of loneliness. You know and understand the desires of my heart, and this brings me comfort to know you only want good for my life, and you will not fail me. Help me to have peace in this process and hope in the wait. Help me to make you the center of my life and to put you first. I ask these blessings in the name of Jesus! Amen.

What things are you currently doing in your life to prepare your heart and soul to receive your soulmate? Based on the reading, what else can you do as you wait for love? Which scripture or scriptures will help you as you wait for love?

_____

_____

_____

_____

_____

Chapter 3: Waiting for Success

Do you feel like you have a God-given assignment, but you have been waiting forever to fulfill it? Has your season of waiting been filled with self-doubt and depression? I ask these questions because, for years, I thought I knew my plan and purpose, and the assignment that I was to complete. Boy, was I wrong! I mapped out my road to success, but there were so many detours along the way. My goals were to obtain a master's degree, and specifically a Specialist's Degree in Curriculum and Instruction. I planned to work my way up the career ladder to become a Curriculum Director in the school system.

I accomplished half of my dream. I now have four degrees, a B.S. in Early Childhood, a Master's in Early Childhood, a Specialist in Curriculum Instruction, Management, and Administration and finally a Doctorate in Education leadership. These degrees, along with several other trainings, have certainly given me the knowledge needed to become a Curriculum Director. I worked hard to earn the degrees, but I have not been able to secure my dream position. For years, this was a big disappointment for me. Although I possessed the confidence and competence needed to fulfill the role, I continued to receive a "no" after each application.

My waiting room for success became filled with selfdoubt and depression. I started wondering if I was good enough. I debated if my training and degrees served any purpose at all. After all the schooling to obtain those degrees, all that

I was left with was a huge student loan debt. I was not even working in a position that paid enough to pay the debt back comfortably. I became complacent and accepted teaching positions with leadership opportunities, but never the final position I desired.

But deep inside, there was always that nudge, a constant reminder that God had a purpose and plan for my life and that I would be successful. I needed to spend more time with God in prayer and meditation on scriptures, asking Him to reveal His plans to me. Do you even know what God's purpose and plans are for your life?

God designed each one of us for a divine purpose. Even before you were formed in your mother's womb, there was a detailed plan for your life. Once you make the connection with God and allow Him to guide you to your purpose, you must believe that no matter what circumstances arise, His plans for you will come to pass.

During my waiting season, I focused on the words in Jeremiah 29:11 (N.I.V.), which state, "'For I know the plans I have for you', declares the Lord, 'plans to prosper you and not to harm you, plans to give you hope and a future.'" This scripture was posted on my mirror in my bathroom so that I would see it every morning and throughout the day as a reminder of what God had promised me.

My idea of prospering was to have an office within the superintendent's department with my name, Dr. Sheila R. Thomas, on the door. I thought my purpose was to assure that the curriculum for reading in the public elementary schools in the county was being implemented to its maximum potential. My passion for reading and phonics instruction was great, and I wanted to be sure every teacher was prepared to reach and teach every child. This seemed to be a great plan, and I had worked hard and received the knowledge I thought was needed to make this happen. But, almost 15 years later, it still had not happened. So, my question was, "What's next?" I prayed and talked to God, family and friends to help me find the answer. Family and friends gave me lots of positive words and encouragement. They helped me to keep pressing on, but a part of me was sinking, plunging into doubt and despair.

Instead of focusing on what others were saying about where I should be in life, I chose to keep my focus on what the word of God means. It states in Psalms 37: 3-4 (K.J.V.), "Trust in the Lord, and do good; so shalt thou dwell in the land, and verily thou shalt be fed. Delight thyself also in the Lord: and he shall give thee the desires of thine heart." I had to repeat this scripture often, trusting and believing that God's plans for me to prosper and make a difference in the field of education would one day come true.

Because the wait was long, and I was not getting the answers I wanted, I took matters into my own hands. I decided to leave teaching in the local public school system and began a job as an Instructor with Albany Technical College. I was happy in my new position, teaching as well as serving as the assistant director for the daycare at Albany Tech for many years, but the work hours were a heavy burden for my family. My husband was also working long hours as well as pastoring a church at the time. We had a baby who also needed my attention at home. Therefore, I decided to take a job at Darton State College for more flexibility. My duties as a Professor and Chairperson for the Early Childhood Department were a relief. Two years later, I was offered the position of Director of Continuing Education. I was satisfied because now, I did not spend most of the day and late evenings at work and was able to be the wife and mother my family needed. Although I genuinely enjoyed both positions, I had abandoned my plan to become a Curriculum Director thinking this was my new career path. During this time, I was not genuinely believing and waiting on God's promise, but instead, I was making decisions based on what I thought was best because things were not happening as quickly as I wanted.

Unexpectedly, after eight years, I had to return to the public school system due to financial issues that were taking place at Darton College. I never planned to return to the local public school as a classroom teacher, but I needed a job. My return as a 4th-grade teacher was not a smooth transition for me. I was an expert when it came to teaching future educators on the philosophy and theory of teaching. However, my instruction did not include many of the new practices (i.e., technology), that was being implemented. It was hard to believe all the changes that had happened in eight years. Students' misbehaviors had become a significant issue in schools. I almost felt like a brand-new teacher and was treated that way. I was required to attend new teacher orientation even though I had over 17 years of teaching experience.

Since I was considered a new teacher, I was not able to apply for the positions that I desired. I felt like I was stuck in the classroom. It was a learning curve for me, plus my heart was not truly there. I loved the children and wanted the best for them. I gave them my best, but at the end of the day, I was not happy. My absence in the school system caused me to lose some of the relationships I once had. There were lots of new people in positions of power. To obtain a higher position, I honestly didn't know the right people. I was heartbroken and felt defeated. I blamed myself for choosing to leave the public school system.

I spent most days just going through the motions of getting up, going to work, coming home and doing it all over again the next day. There was no joy or peace in my heart. I came to a place where I would wail to God to deliver me from this feeling of defeat. This emotional state was taking a toll on my body and my family. I was miserable, and it was seeping into my relationship with my husband and son. I was always tired, bitter, angry, snappy and moody at home. I knew I had to find some peace. I continued to pray for it daily.

I started repeating the verse in Romans 8:28 (K.J.V.), which says, "And we know that God works all things together for the good of those who love Him, who are called according to *His* purpose." I started to believe that the position I was in was purposeful. I realized that I was not only touching the lives of many children but was asked to serve as a mentor to other teachers everywhere I taught. In these positions, I had the opportunity to impart knowledge about the curriculum, share ways to eliminate student behaviors, as well as ways to help new teachers to stay motivated.

I was not a Curriculum Director, but I was certainly making a positive impact on the curriculum within my control. For years, I traveled across the state providing research-based trainings to daycare providers. I had also served as an Intervention Specialist, lead teacher, and member of the leadership team at my various schools. These roles were opportunities to make decisions alongside administrators that affected instruction and student growth. On the college level, I was chairperson and student advisor, and in these positions, I was the one to make any changes needed in the curriculum for students. As the assistant director for the daycare, I was the one who reviewed teachers' lesson plans and implemented programs for the parents. Finally, as Director of Continuing Education, I created a catalog of courses for the community. These roles and activities definitely impacted the curriculum in many ways.

Once I realized that God was using me and was also allowing me to complete other goals, such as becoming an author and educational consultant and being able to have time at home to nurture my family, I came to a sense of peace. Instead of wallowing in what I thought was a failure, I decided to use this as a learning experience. I gained renewed strength that I could do the job, and as Paul states in Philippians 4:12-13 (N.I.V.), I have learned the secret of being content in any and every situation. I can do all this through Him who gives me strength.

Winning or losing is influenced by the way we live and think. We have the power to determine how our story will unfold. God has given us a divine connection through prayer that will help to create our future. We must lean into God for understanding and ask Him to reveal His plans for our life.

While you are in the waiting room, having a positive attitude, and seeking God are the keys to your success. This attitude includes trusting God and declaring positive affirmations that you will live a successful life. Every day is a gift, and we must determine what we will do with it to meet our goals. We must spend each day with God, praying and listening to His directions for our purpose in life. Living life with complacency or in a rut is an equation for destruction. A woeful spirit stops a person from moving forward and causes them to blame others. Instead, a person needs to do as the word says in Philippians 4:13 (K.J.V.) and press toward the mark of the prize of the high calling of God in Christ Jesus. Staying focused by walking and talking with God daily will keep your attitude positive while in the waiting room for success. Choose wisely. The road to success includes placing your hope in God to renew your strength. You can soar like an eagle, run and not grow weary, walk, and not faint. While in the waiting room for success, speak positive affirmations on your life as you prepare to step out of the waiting room and into a life of success.

Take delight in the Lord, and he will give you your heart's desires. Waiting for success may take months, years, or even decades, but choosing to believe His word and apply the principles written in the Bible to your life will make the waiting room a more comfortable place to be. Stay connected to God and let go of your plans. Walk and talk with Him daily and never stray from Him. Ask Him for what you want, and He will listen and give you the desires of your heart. Ask Him to show you your purpose. Make your request known to Him. Luke 11: 9 (K.J.V.) reads, "And I say, Ask, and it shall be given you; seek and ye shall find; knock, and it shall be opened unto you." Embrace these words for confirmation that God will give you the desires of your heart. Sometimes the time spent in the waiting room may be long, but God is gracious and generous with His promises. While waiting, spend time walking and talking with Him to make that great connection, and soon your prayers will be answered.

Don't give up on your dreams. Paul tells us in Galatians 6:9 (N.I.V.), "Let us not become weary in doing good, for at the proper time we will reap a harvest if we don't give up." Don't give up on God, because He won't give up on you. He is able and willing to give you all that He has promised. Keep believing, trusting and walking with Him.

While in the waiting room for success, read and meditate on the following scriptures and pray the prayer below.

Now faith is the substance of things hoped for, the evidence of things not seen. Hebrews 11:1 (K.J.V.)

And observe what the Lord your God requires: Walk in his ways, and keep his decrees and commands, his laws and requirements, as written in the Law of Moses, so that you may prosper in all you do and wherever you go. Kings 2:3 (N.I.V.)

Commit to the Lord whatever you do, and he will establish your plans. Proverbs 16:3 (N.I.V.)

I can do all this through him who gives me strength. Philippians 4:13 (N.I.V.)

So do not fear, for I am with you; do not be dismayed, for I am your God. I will strengthen and help you; I will uphold you with my righteous right hand. Isaiah 41:10 (N.I.V.)

But blessed is the man who trusts in the Lord, whose confidence is in him. Jeremiah 17:7 (N.I.V.)

My son, forget not my law; but let thine heart keep my commandments: For length of days, and long life, and peace, shall they add to thee. Let not mercy and truth forsake thee: bind them about thy neck; write them upon the table of thine heart: So shalt thou find favour and good understanding in the sight of God and man. Proverbs 3:14 (K.J.V.)

Humble yourselves in the sight of the Lord, and he shall lift you up. James 4:10 (K.J.V.)

And we know that all things work together for good to them that love God, to them who are the called according to his purpose. Romans 8:28 (K.J.V.)

Prayer for Success

Heavenly Father, I know you have an excellent plan for my life. You promised in your word to give me a great future. I do not know exactly what my future looks like, but I trust whatever you have planned because if you are in it, it is good. I pray for patience and to not give up and trust You during moments when I feel negative emotions. Help me not to take matters in my own hands. Deepen my understanding and give me greater knowledge of what You are doing in my life.

Help me to pray by faith, believe, wait and then move forward in Your timing. I pray you would lift me out when I slip into worry, sadness, or fear, and remind me of your goodness and grace. Help me seek you above my every hope, desire and dreams for myself. Fill me with your peace and joy and continue to remind me that You are working all things out for my good. Thank you so much for your love and care. In Jesus' Name, Amen.

Are you completely trusting God for your success? Why or why not? Do you believe that all things that have happened in your time of waiting have been for your good? Why or why not? Based on your reading, what must you do to bring contentment during your wait for success?

_____

_____

_____

_____

_____

Chapter 4: Waiting for a Financial Breakthrough

For many years, my family and I struggled to pay bills and to keep enough money in our account for our wants and emergencies. Our finances were totally out of control, and we were spending more money than we were earning. Reaching a level of financial security and being debt-free had always been one of my life goals. To achieve this goal of becoming debt-free and having enough in store to bless my church and others, we had to take control of our spending. We needed financial counseling from someone who knew money and knew exactly how to use it wisely. I listened to Dave Ramsey, watched Susie Orman, consulted with a couple of financial advisors. Still, most importantly, I prayed for wisdom and guidance to help dig my family out of this hole of debt. Deuteronomy 8:18 (K.J.V.) says, "We shalt remember the Lord thy God: for it is he that giveth thee power to get wealth, that he may establish his covenant which he sware unto thy fathers, as it is this day." It has taken several years to become a disciplined spender and saver, and I still have a long way to go, but now my bank account looks a lot better after the bills have been paid.

During the first couple of years of my marriage, our finances were stable. We only had one car payment, which we were able to pay off in a year. We were then left with a house note, essential house bills such as electricity, insurance, phone bills, cable and daycare. It was nice to have extra money left over to buy the things we sometimes wanted. Our first financial mishap was buying something I desired but could not really afford. I always said that I wanted a Mercedes for my 40th birthday. Remember when I told you that I was my husband's Queen? Well, guess what? My husband bought me a white Mercedes Benz 350 on my birthday. The payment was not exceptionally high, but it was still more than we should have put into a car. To top it off, it turned out to be a lemon, anyway. The following year, we purchased vehicles for both of our sons. Although their car payments were low, it still began to put a strain on our income. We also were still spending on our wants instead of being cautious with money. This was when our finances began to spiral out of control.

The bills were steadily piling up from three different car notes, credit cards and personal loans. There were also bills from doctor visits and medications. My husband and I had rather good combined salaries, but we owed almost more than what we were bringing in. We paid the bills, but any leftover money was quickly spent on our wants. We were struggling, but you could not tell by looking at us. We looked the part and played it well.

At the beginning of every new year, I have always heard the same messages of prosperity. "This is your year for a bountiful blessing. You will have an overflow of money this year. You will be the lender and not the borrower!" I have been prophesied over many times that the upcoming year would be my year of blessings and financial overflow. When I would hear these words, I would get excited, thinking about all the money I would have, and what I would buy. I considered tax season the time for my biggest monetary blessing. I always knew that during the month of February, March, or April, I was going to get a significant income tax refund check. I always made plans on how I would spend it even before it was processed by the I.R.S. I did not even think about saving money for a rainy day. I spent all of it, most of the time, within a couple of weeks of receiving the direct deposit. I was that foolish woman in Proverbs 14:1 (N.I.V.), tearing down my house with my spending habits. I did pay a few bills, but the majority was spent on clothes, shoes and food. After the income tax checks had come and gone, my bank account would return to its usual status of being extremely low or even overdrawn.

This was my family's norm for years. We were still functioning in this roller coaster of debt when we finally paid off the boys' cars. You would think we would have been smart enough to not add any additional expenses once we had eliminated two car notes. Please! We decided to trade in my Mercedes, which was becoming a money pit. Instead of downsizing, I upgraded and got a brand-new BMW with a higher payment. Although the payment was higher, I did not care because it was what I really wanted. Money was not an object. We were paying my car note plus daycare fees, college fees for our son and loaning money to family and friends who thought we had it to spare. Two years later, my husband decided it was his turn to get a new vehicle, and he opted for a fully loaded brand new Ford F-150. This added payment and the increased cost of insurance crushed us.

The next five years were devastating! Credit card bills increased, car payments fell behind and our bank account was always at a bare minimum or overdrawn. On top of all this, we relocated to a new city. What a bind we were in! We were paying the mortgage for the house we left and paying rent in our new city. It took three years before the house finally sold. Still, we looked like we had it all together. What a nightmare! Something had to change. I wanted things to get better, but I was still robbing Peter to pay Paul. I was paying off one credit card to pay another or paying bills with credit cards. We continued to stay in debt. I would open new credit cards for the lower interest and free rate promotions, but most of the time, I was not able to pay the card off before the interest-free period was up.

The most nerve-racking part of being financially unstable was when the bank account was overdrawn or at a bare minimum, and an emergency would arise. It was also dèjá vu of the days growing up and listening to my mom haggle with debt collectors on the phone. Now, I was doing the same thing. I avoided answering my phone. When I did, I was often negotiating with bill collectors. Something had to give. This was not a good life, and it kept me feeling stressed and panicky.

Meanwhile, on the outside, I was driving my brand-new BMW, wearing cute clothes, and my nails and hair were always done. I was living a lie. The bills kept stacking up, but I continued to rack up on things by using credit cards for purchases or borrowing from loan companies. We had an image to uphold since I had a doctoral degree, and my husband was a manager and pastor. Keeping up with the lifestyle of some friends and family members was a must. Therefore, my spending was to make me and my family look and feel good, and for others to see us as prosperous.

When my finances continued to plunge, there were times I questioned whether God planned to bless me with more than enough. I often asked where the was manifestation He promised? How much longer must I wait for my bountiful portion? I felt myself slipping into a state of depression. I began to lose my passion for work, and my joy at home was fading. I was like a hamster on a wheel. I worked every day, but my finances were never getting better. I had now come to a low and desperate point for help. My only option left was to pray and listen to what God told me to do to break free from this burden of debt. By going to God in prayer, I asked Him to show me how to live a better life financially. I vowed to listen for His response during my daily moments of silence. He revealed that He was indeed blessing me while taking care of my wants, needs and some desires. He also showed me that I was the problem.

Initially, I thought that I was the sole reason our bank account spiraled to a bare minimum month after month. The choices I had made to buy expensive cars, shopping and eating out often were all bad choices. God spoke to me, and it also became clear that I was not alone carrying the weight of my family's financial despair. My husband was also part of the problem. Although we combined our income each pay period, he was not a full participant when it was time to make decisions and pay bills. He was very relaxed about money, and his idea of contributing to the household finances was to work hard and give me access to whatever money he made. His thoughts were that I had everything under control, and all he needed was food, electricity and something to drive. I pleaded with him often to assist me each month as I paid bills, but he was not willing to take part. This was a problem. We were unequally yoked when it came to money matters. I appreciated the trust he placed in me, but as the years went by and the bills started piling up more and more, it became overwhelming, causing me to become distressed and even angry.

I was now frustrated. I knew that I could not continue to handle this financial burden alone. I desperately needed my husband's help. My prayer to God was for Him to open my husband's heart and mind to become my helpmate with the finances. In distress, I cried out to God to give me the words to say to my husband so that he could understand the situation. The moment of breakthrough for my husband came on his job. He was at work the day I went to buy groceries at the store that he manages. I could feel the weight on my shoulders as I mentally calculated how much I could spend that day. He was standing at the front entrance of the store and could see the distress on my face. As soon as he asked me what was wrong, I broke down in tears and explained to him how keeping up with the finances was a heavy burden, and I needed his help. Seeing me in this state was a reality check for him. He never knew how stressful the financial situation had gotten until he saw me at this low point.

That is when my husband joined with me to gain an understanding of our financial situation and what we needed to do to dig ourselves out of debt. Taking care of the home became our number one priority. We were often lending money and paying bills for others when we really did not have it. We both were guilty of not consulting with each other before lending money to others. This also sometimes caused conflict in our home. We agreed to bless others in need only if we were able to sacrifice without expectation for the money to be returned. Now, when someone asks either one of us to borrow money or pay a bill, we discuss what's in the account and what household bills need to be taken care of first. This helps us to ensure that we are able to live comfortably even if the money is not returned.

From that point until now, we continue to discuss our spending and lending habits and focus on how we should work as partners to make our finances better. We consulted with a financial counselor and created a plan to get out of debt. Most importantly, we prayed for wisdom and guidance from God to show us the right path to financial freedom. After making our commitment to each other and the Lord to work together to better our finances, our eyes were opened to our financial priorities. We vowed to give our tithes faithfully every month, some months even going over and beyond our expectations. We knew that God had blessed us and would continue to bless us not just financially, but in all areas of life.

My husband and I have waited a long time to see our bank account have a positive balance every month after the bills were paid. Being on one accord is what was missing to have financial prosperity. We now sit together monthly and set goals for paying bills, our spending for weekly meals and planning how much to set aside for future expenses and financial emergencies that may arise. We also discuss money matters with our youngest child, who still lives at home, giving him an understanding of the how's and why's of money. Since he is more involved and has a better understanding of money, he now limits the things he asks from us. These strategies of praying, paying bills together and consulting each other in all areas of our spending has become our new routine. After months of this teamwork, things have drastically improved. Paying bills is no longer a burden to me because I now have a partner who helps to carry the weight.

Couples must be open with each other about finances and work together to strengthen their relationship with money matters in order to meet financial goals. I encourage others to consult with a financial advisor, set goals for spending and give your tithes. Financial freedom is possible for anyone, and it does not depend on how much money you make, but instead, it depends on the choices you make with the money you have. Make good financial choices, and you will see the benefits. Waiting for a financial breakthrough was stressful and sometimes discouraging, but we kept the faith knowing that God is a provider. God provides us with more than enough to be debt-free, but we must be good stewards of what we have. Luke 1:37 (N.I.V.) tells us that nothing is impossible for God. It is possible that the mountain of debt you have accumulated can be knocked down if you pray, trust God and do the work necessary to tackle it. His promise to us may is found in Mark 11:23 (N.I.V.) which reads, "Truly I tell you, if anyone says to this mountain, 'Go, throw yourself into the sea,' and does not doubt in their heart but believes that what they say will happen, it will be done for them." Pray, trust, believe, do the necessary work, and eventually, God will bring you out of the waiting room of debt and into financial freedom.

While in the waiting room for a financial breakthrough, read and meditate on the following scriptures and recite the prayer below.

Give, and it will be given to you. A good measure, pressed down, shaken together and running over, will be poured into your lap. For with the measure you use, it will be measured to you. Luke 6:38 (N.I.V.)

Now unto him that is able to do exceeding abundantly above all that we ask or think, according to the power that worketh in us. "*Ephesians 3:20 (K.J.V.)

Whoever can be trusted with very little can also be trusted with much, and whoever is dishonest with very little will also be dishonest with much. So if you have not been trustworthy in handling worldly wealth, who will trust you with true riches? Luke 16:10-11 (N.I.V.)

But remember the Lord your God, for it is he who gives you the ability to produce wealth, and so confirms his covenant, which he swore to your ancestors, as it is today. Deuteronomy 8:18 (N.I.V.)

Wealth and riches shall be in his house: and his righteousness endureth forever. Psalms 112:3 (K.J.V.)

The lions may grow weak and hungry, but those who seek the Lord lack no good thing. Psalms 34:10 (N.I.V.)

Bring the whole tithe into the storehouse, that there may be food in my house. Test me in this, says the Lord

Almighty, and see if I will not throw open the floodgates of heaven and pour out so much blessing that there will not be room enough to store it. I will prevent pests from devouring your crops, and the vines in your fields will not drop their fruit before it is ripe, says the Lord Almighty. Then all the nations will call you blessed, for yours will be a delightful land, says the Lord Almighty. Malachi 3:10 (N.I.V.)

But my God shall supply all your needs according to his riches in glory by Christ Jesus. Philippians 4:19 (K.J.V.)

Prayer for Financial Freedom

Lord, I come to you with a heart full of thanksgiving, recognizing that every good gift and perfect gift comes from You. I ask that You place Your hand on my finances. I need You to fix my life so that I will be prosperous and have more than enough to give to your kingdom and others. Thank You, Lord, for blessing my family with money to spend. I believe that my family and I will have a lack of nothing. I trust your wisdom and guidance for creative ideas and opportunities to build wealth to leave a legacy for my children's children. My family and I will remain faithful in giving our tithes and be givers not only financially, but with the gifts and talents you have given us. I pray that you will not only protect our finances, but you will also cause our finances to overflow. We rebuke the spirit of lack and trust that every dollar you have for us is ours. Thank You for providing for us, and I thank You for all that You've done and all that You're going to do. In the name of Jesus, I pray! Amen!

What steps are you currently taking to improve your finances? What is working and not working? From your reading, what steps can you add while you wait?

_____
_____
_____
_____
_____
_____
_____
_____
_____
_____
_____
_____
_____
_____
_____
_____

W.A.I.T Women Anticipating Incredible Turnaround

Final Thoughts

Waiting can sometimes be painful and frustrating, but you must walk in faith and be encouraged during the waiting period. Sometimes, we get anxious, impatient or moody when it is our turn to demonstrate self-restraint. But just as we tell children to wait, our Heavenly Father sometimes makes us wait. He puts us in a waiting room for a purpose, and He is not always in a hurry to release us. Our wait is to purge us, transform us, and most importantly, to develop our relationship with Him. It is a time when a woman must practice self-control and regulate her mind. When times get tough, keep pushing, ask others for help, but never give up. The letters in the word, "PUSH" are commonly associated with the acronym Pray. Until. Something. Happens. Prayer is the divine connection to the Father. He wants to hear from you, and He wants to talk to you. Take time to listen to what He has to say. Jesus wants to walk with you and wants you to enjoy the moment and journey with Him by your side. Just like Jesus was in the fiery furnace with the Hebrew boys and the lion's den with Daniel, He is also in the waiting room with you.

God has a purpose for placing us in the waiting room. Even Jesus, whose ultimate sacrifice was to die for our sins, had to wait to fulfill His promise. Jesus gives us the perfect example of what to do while waiting. He shows us how to pray and continue to walk towards our destiny. Our purpose has been set before us, but it may take days, months or years before we reach it. During this time, we must pray without ceasing, serve others and not grumble or complain.

Trust God while in your waiting room and know that He is directing your steps and preparing you for your next destination. A woman must think positive thoughts about what is to come while in the waiting room. God will release you from the period of waiting once He knows that your heart is in the right place, and you are ready to receive the blessing He has in store for you. Never take your eyes off the prize; but instead, focus on what He has promised. ***"Let us hold unswervingly to the hope we profess, for HE who has promised us is faithful." Hebrews 10:23 (N.I.V.)***

During your wait time for healing, surround yourself with like-minded people who will help you stay accountable during the journey. Release all pain, hurt and disappointment so that you can take control of your life. Let others pour into you, and you should also pour your spiritual truths in others. Become a servant and watch how God will heal your spirit and bring you an incredible turnaround. For those who are waiting for healing from physical pains or grieving a loved one, Jesus will bring you joy as He states in John 16: 22-23 (N.K.J.V.), "Therefore, you now have sorrow, but I will see you again, and your heart will rejoice, and your joy no one will take from you. And on that day, you will ask Me nothing. Most assuredly,

I say to you, whatever you ask the Father in My name, He will give you". Jesus will provide you with peace and comfort during your wait for healing.

While waiting for love and marriage, get to know yourself first. Discover the things that you need to change so that God can connect you with your soulmate. Do not rush the process of waiting for that person who you plan to spend the rest of your life with. In His timing, He will allow an incredible turnaround to occur in your love life. With God, there is not an appointed time; and if it is a true gift from God, it is worth the wait. "For the vision is yet for an appointed time, but at the end, it shall speak, and not lie: though it tarry, wait for it; because it will surely come, it will not tarry." Habakkuk 2:3 (K.J.V.).

Waiting for success was one of the biggest struggles in my life. This journey of waiting was so hard because I had a plan of what defined a successful career for me, but God's plan was different. "'For I know the plans I have for you,' declares the LORD, 'plans to prosper you and not to harm you, plans to give you hope and a future.'" Jeremiah 29:11 (N.I.V.). While waiting patiently for your success, you should honor God where you are in your career. Embrace where you are, pray, listen for His word and expect an incredible turnaround.

No matter how big your mountain of debt may be, remember that God is bigger. Eliminating debt can seem like a difficult task, especially when you tackle it alone.

What worked for my husband and I was to attack it together and to include God in our financial decisions. Apostle Paul states in Philippians 4:19 (K.J.V.), "But my God shall supply all your need according to his riches in glory by Christ Jesus." God intends for us to live a prosperous life, not just in terms of material things, but to have joy, peace and live a life of comfort. God wants His children to be blessed!

My prayer is that you find peace during the process of *Waiting for Your Incredible Turnaround*. While in your waiting room, do not grow weary or tired. Those who wait on the Lord in expectancy will gain new strength and power. Instead of crying over what God is carrying you through, praise Him in advance for the manifestations that will happen in your life. Even when you can't see it working out, trust God. Remember that all things work together for good for those who love God. If you are broken, let God do the mending. Put God first and watch how your life changes.

It is my hope and prayer that your Wait for an Incredible Turnaround is filled with joy and peace. While you wait, use that time to strengthen your faith and draw closer to God. Trust and believe in His word for in Psalms 130:5 (K.J.V.), it says, "I wait for the Lord, my soul doth wait, and in his word do I hope." The words in Psalm 37:3-4 have been a comfort for my soul and I hope they provide peace for you as well. "Trust in the Lord, and do good; so shalt thou dwell in the land, and verily thou shalt be fed. Delight thyself also in the Lord; and He shall give thee the desires of thine heart."

"And we know that all things work together for good to them that love God, to them who are the called according to his purpose." Romans 8:28 (N.I.V.) "For nothing will be impossible with God." Luke 1:37(ESV). Wait and Anticipate your Incredible Turnaround!

www.ingramcontent.com/pod-product-compliance
Lightning Source LLC
Chambersburg PA
CBHW081236080526
44587CB00022B/3953